D1413072

HOW TO
LAND ON YOUR FEET
LIFE LESSONS FROM MY CAT

Illustrated by Jamie Shelman

THE EXPERIMENT

NEW YORK

The Experiment, LLC
220 East 23rd Street, Suite 600
New York, NY 10010-4658
theexperimentpublishing.com

The Experiment's books are available at special discounts when purchased in bulk for premiums and sales promotions as well as for fund-raising or educational use. For details, contact us at info@theexperimentpublishing.com.

Library of Congress Cataloging-in-Publication Data available upon request

ISBN 978-1-61519-592-3
Ebook ISBN 978-1-61519-593-0

Cover design by Beth Bugler
Text design by Claire Cater

Manufactured in China

First printing September 2019
10 9 8 7 6 5 4 3 2 1

DEDICATED TO MY NEIGHBOR'S CAT,
BROOKSY, WHO WAITS FOR US EVERY
MORNING AT OUR WINDOW

I have loved and lived with many cats throughout my life, and know there are many lessons to be learned from watching our feline friends: from how to get what you want, to being at peace with yourself, to knowing what matters most in life ... food, sleep, and a little companionship!

In this fast-paced, distracted world, now more than ever I find myself turning to cats (mostly my neighbor's, Brooksy) for comfort, quietude, joy, and even a little guidance. Cats are wise and silly, needy and aloof, simple and unique—and oh-so-brilliant at doing nothing. I hope that, in this book, you recognize some of the lessons you've learned from your own cat—and that one day we can all learn to sit perfectly still, eyes squinted with pleasure, content until the next meal!

—Jamie

STRETCH REGULARLY

GET PLENTY OF REST

. . . BECAUSE NAPS ARE
NEVER TO BE ASHAMED OF

STAY WARM

ENJOY YOUR QUIET TIME

MAINTAIN A
WELL-GROOMED APPEARANCE

EAT MORE FISH

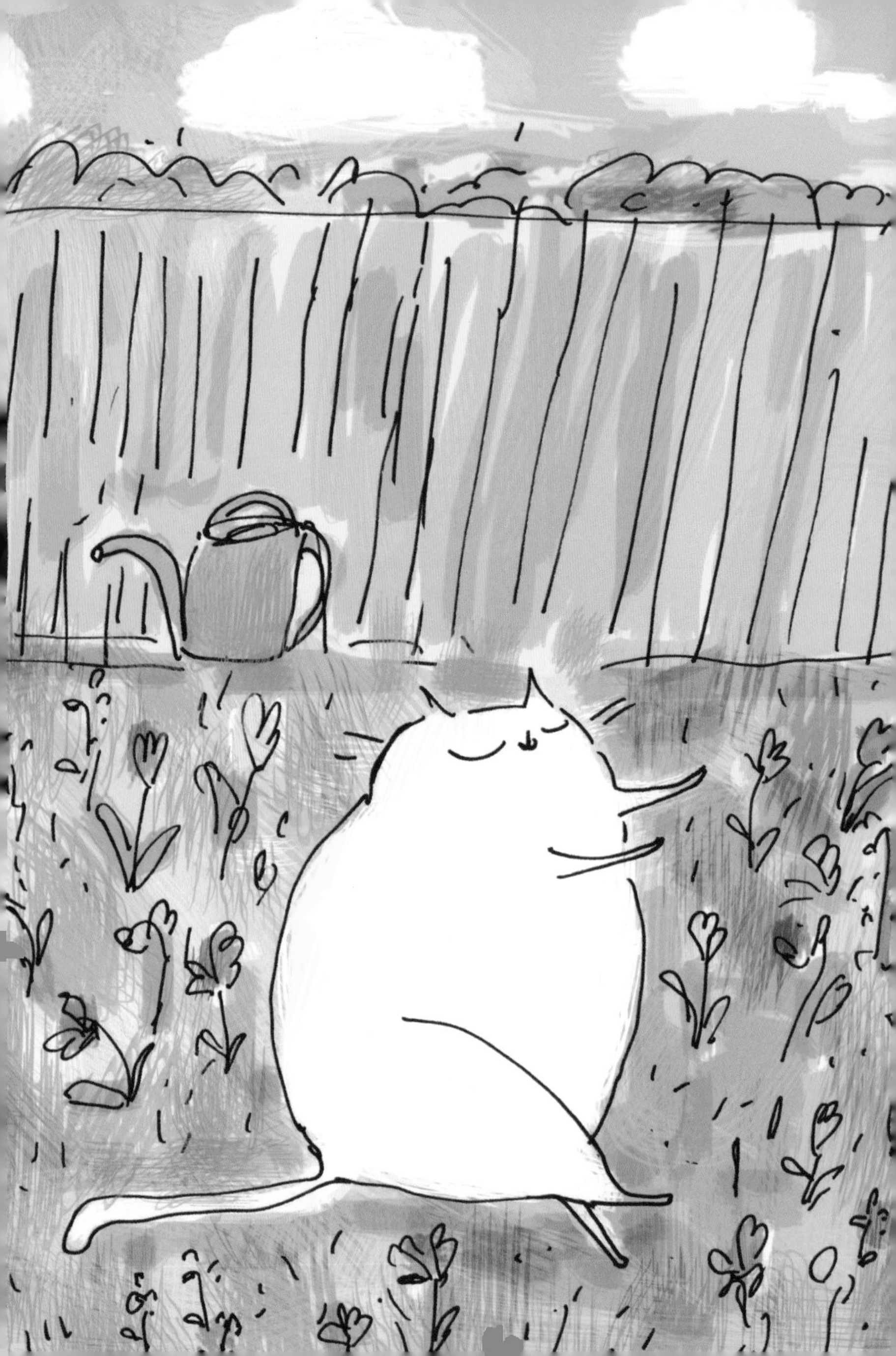

SOAK UP THE SUN

EAT ONLY WHAT YOU WANT

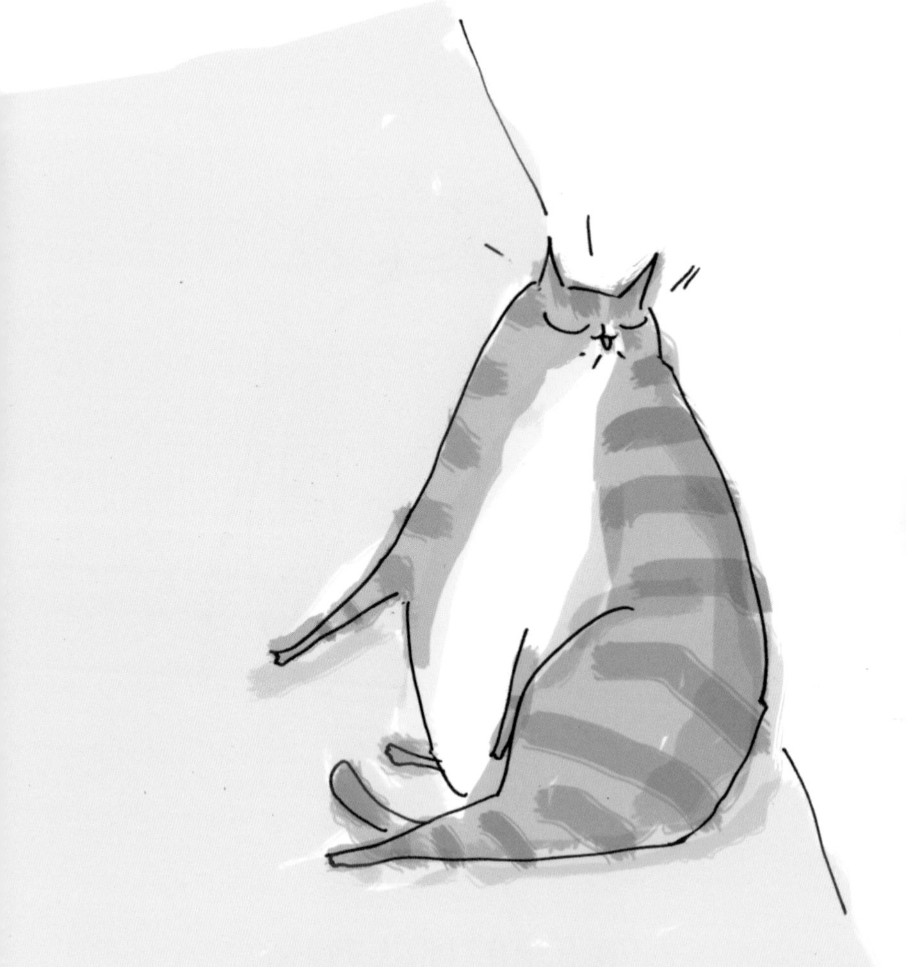

WASH WHEN YOU CAN

A BEAUTIFUL MANE
TAKES SERIOUS WORK

. . . AND SO DOES THE
PERFECT SET OF NAILS

BE AN EARLY RISER

... BUT IT'S OK TO SLEEP IN
NOW AND THEN

DAYDREAM EXTRAVAGANTLY

SPEAK UP WHEN YOU
NEED SOMETHING

CONSERVE YOUR ENERGY

THINK

OUTSIDE

THE BOX

BE PATIENT

. . . AND KEEP YOUR EYE ON THE PRIZE

PRACTICE THE ART OF NEGOTIATION

BE DIRECT

GIVE POSITIVE FEEDBACK

MAKE EYE CONTACT

SHRED ALL DOCUMENTS

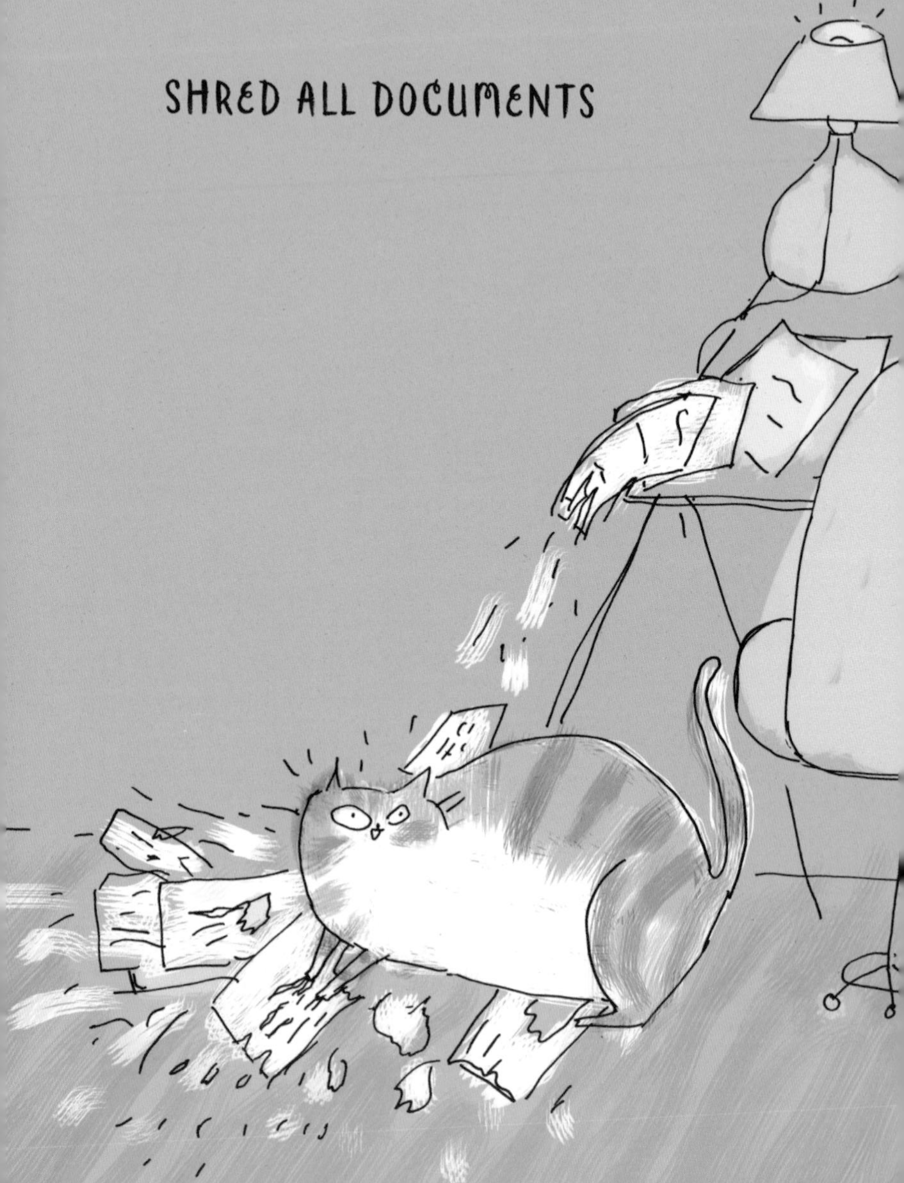

DON'T BE DISCOURAGED

DON'T
WORK TOO
HARD

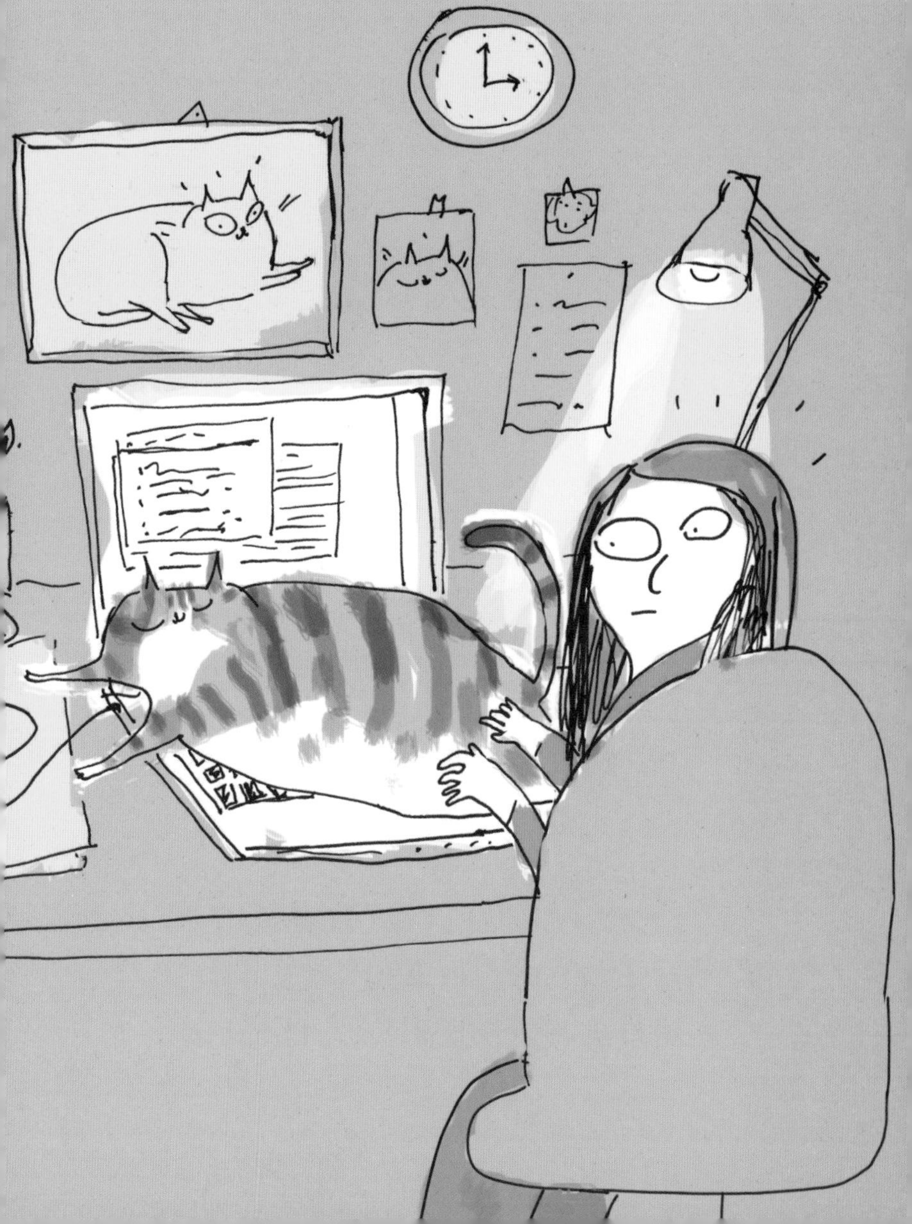

BE ESPECIALLY ATTENTIVE
TO THE ONE PERSON IN THE
ROOM WHO DOESN'T LIKE YOU

BE PLEASED WITH YOUR ACHIEVEMENTS, HOWEVER SMALL

PURRFECT YOUR DEATH STARE

PURRFECT YOUR POKER FACE

MAKE

YOUR

MARK

WALK WITH (C)ATTITUDE

. . . AND KEEP THE CLAWS SHARP

STAY FOCUSED

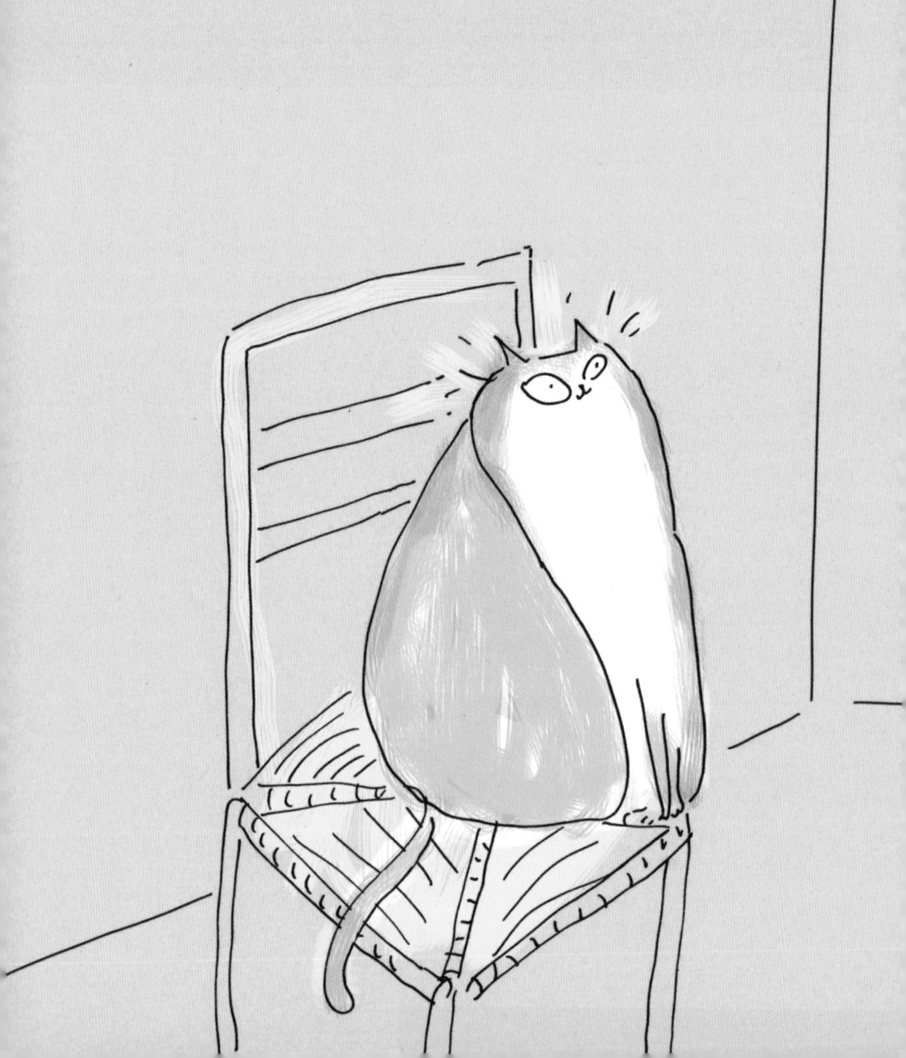

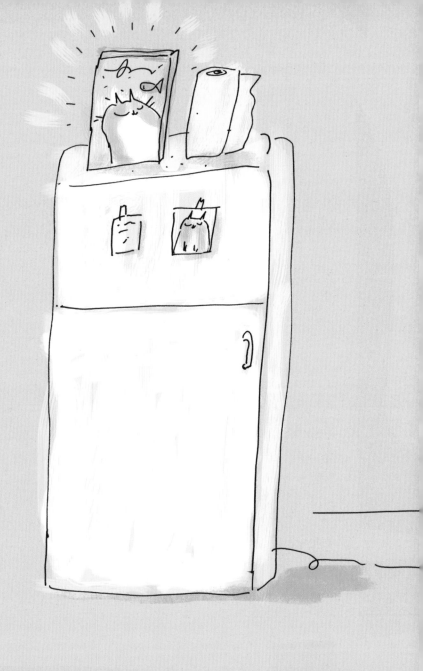

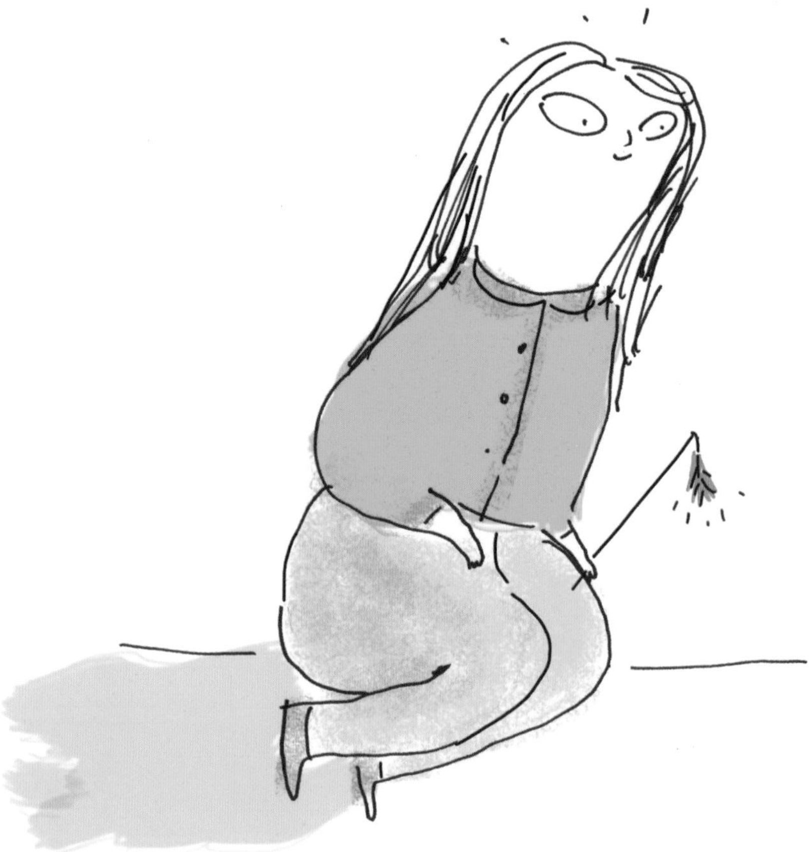

ONCE YOU'VE MADE UP YOUR MIND, DON'T CHANGE IT

AIM HIGH

THE BEST SOLUTION TO A
PROBLEM IS A NAP

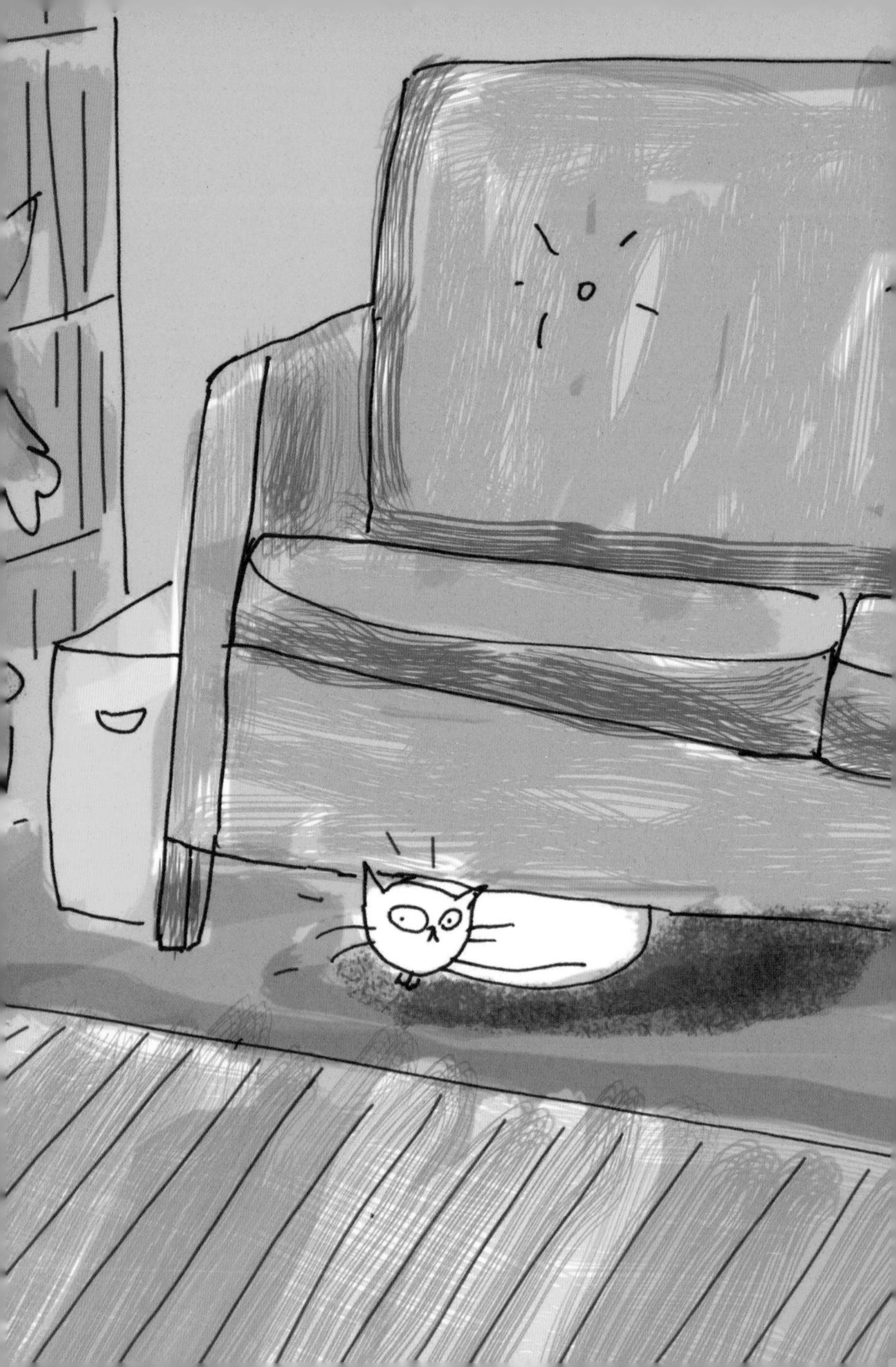

ANXIETY IS NOTHING TO BE ASHAMED OF

LIVE IN THE MOMENT

BE RESILIENT

DON'T SWEAT THE SMALL STUFF

IT'S OK TO BE ANTISOCIAL

TAKE TIME TO REFLECT

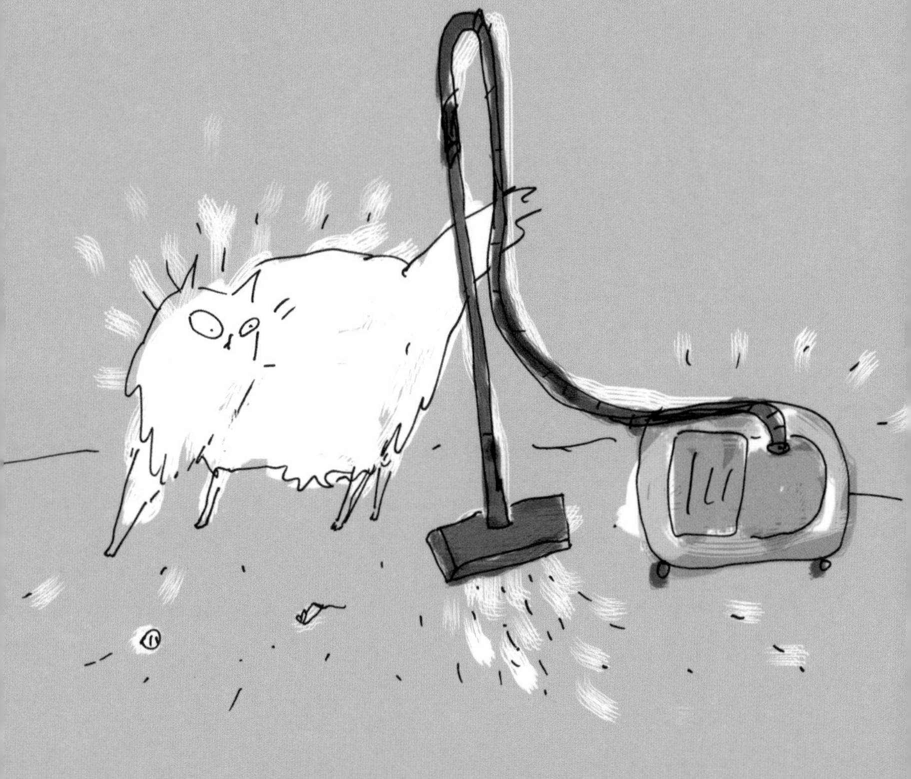

CONFRONT YOUR FEARS

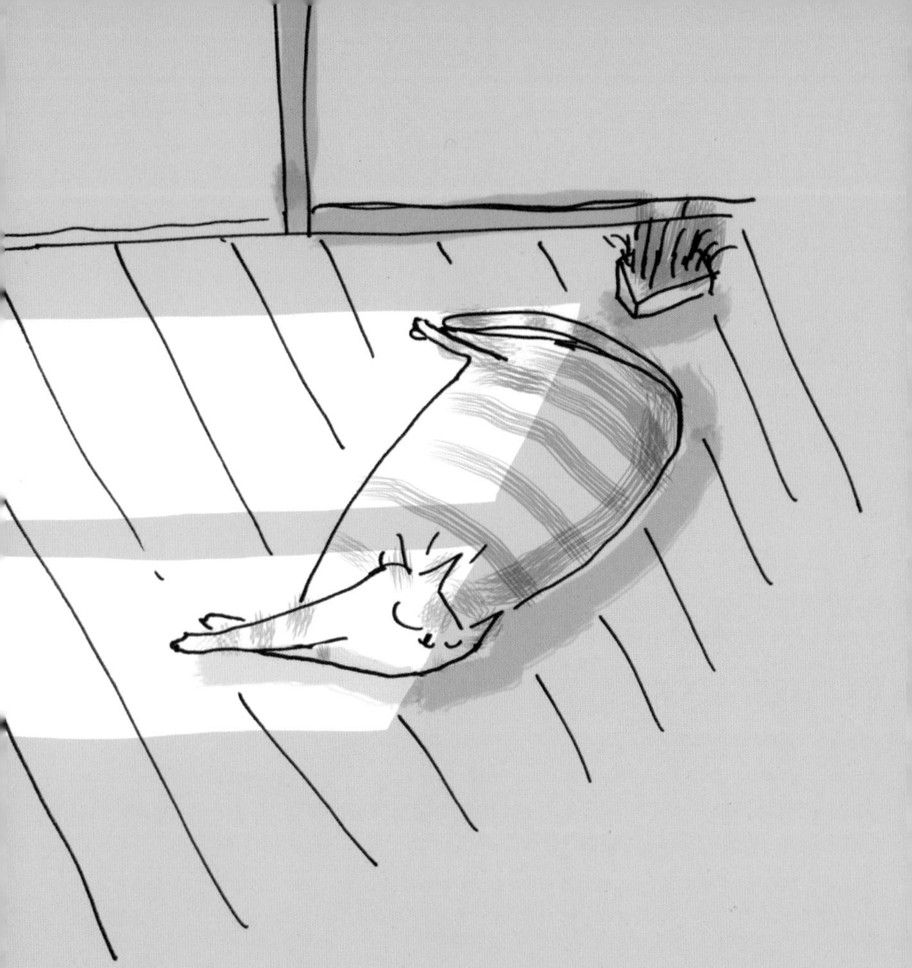

SLOW DOWN

EXERCISE ONLY WHEN YOU FEEL LIKE IT

LIVE OUTSIDE YOUR COMFORT ZONE

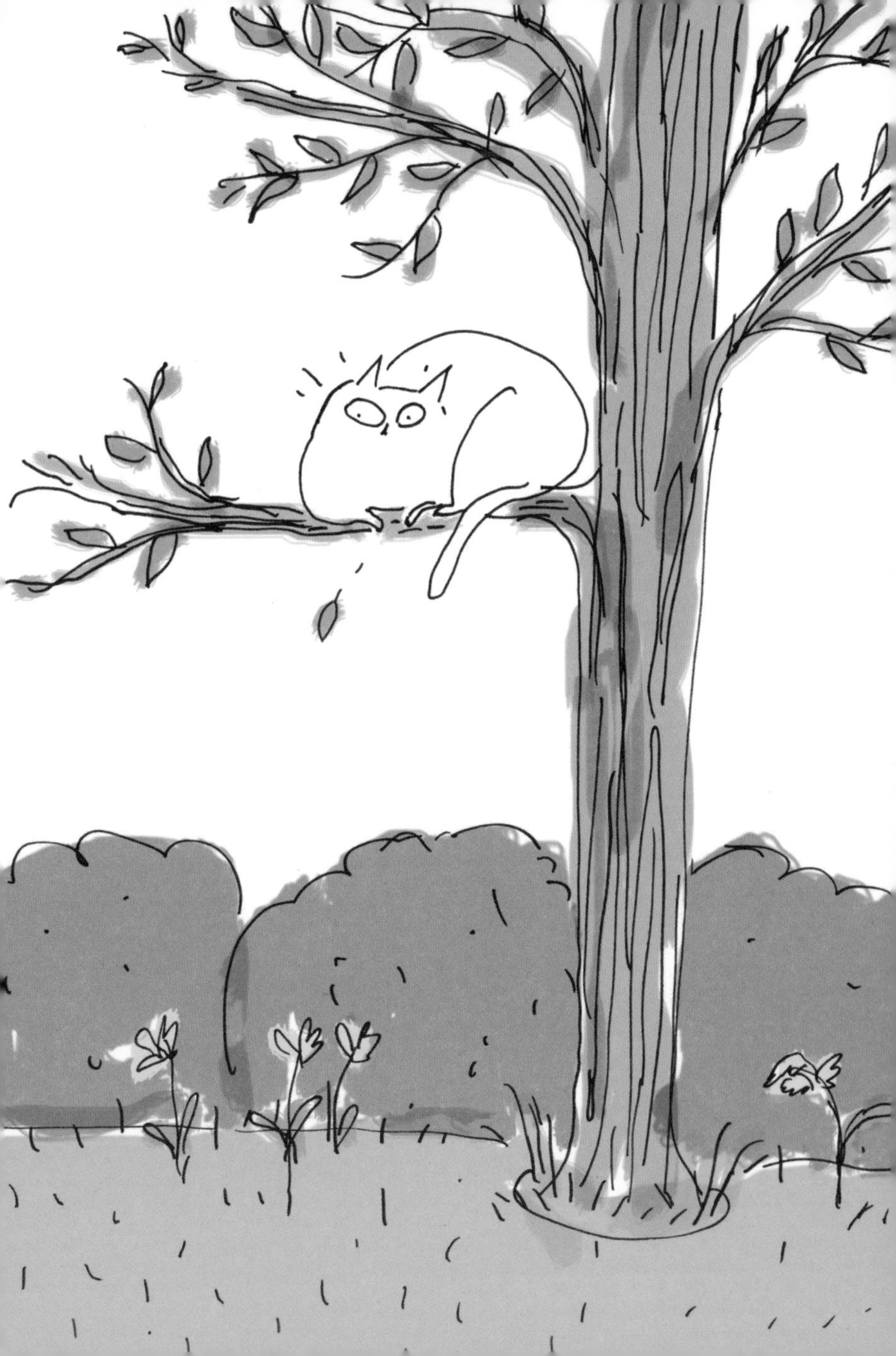

NOTHING IS PERSONAL

IRRATIONAL FEARS ARE NORMAL

MAKE THE MOST OF
WHAT YOU'VE GOT

DRINKING WATER IS
GOOD FOR THE SOUL

LOOK AFTER YOURSELF FIRST

DON'T BE AFRAID TO LET SOMEONE
KNOW THAT YOU LIKE THEM

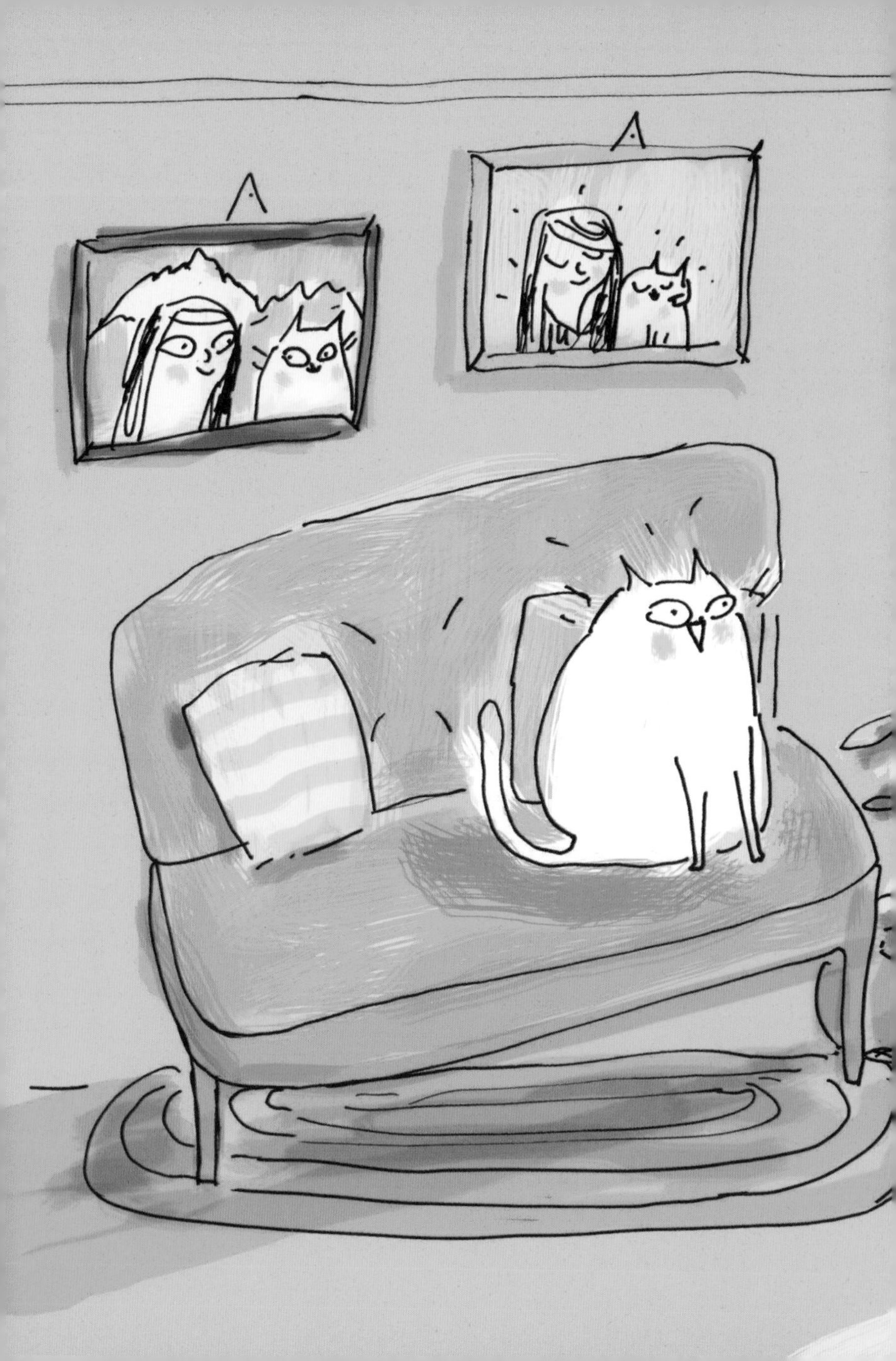

ALWAYS LOOK PLEASED WHEN
THEY COME THROUGH THE DOOR

BE WHO YOU ARE
AND THE RIGHT
PERSON WILL
LOVE YOU FOR IT

BE GOOD AT RECEIVING AFFECTION

. . . BUT DON'T BE NEEDY

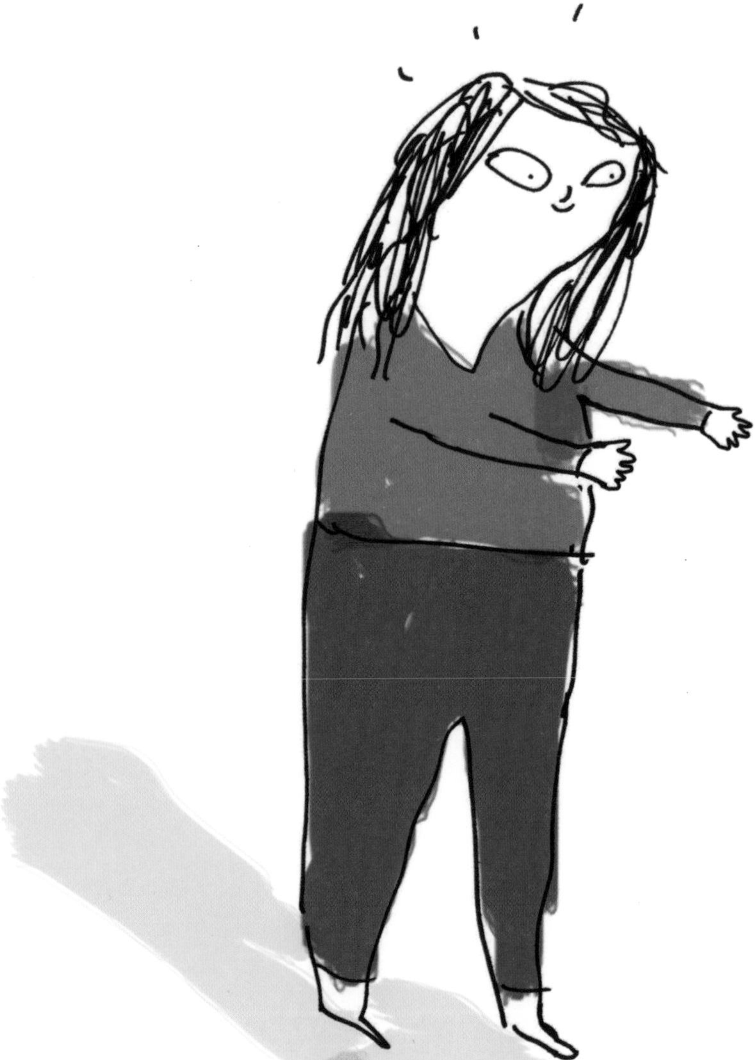

STAY AT LEAST TEN FEET AWAY FROM
YOUR LOVED ONE AT ALL TIMES

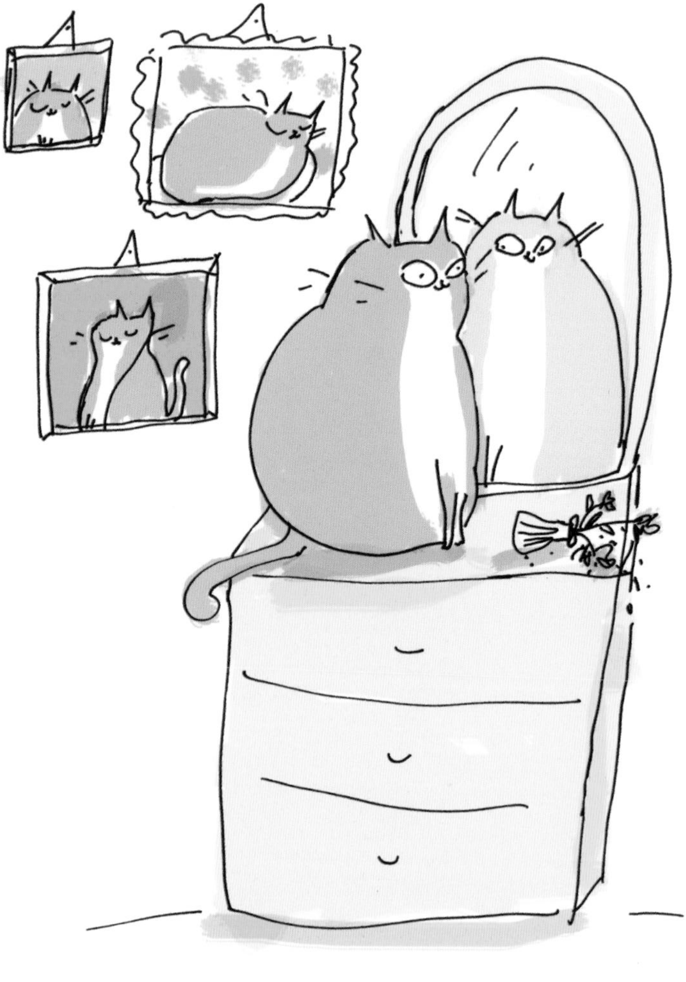

LOVE YOURSELF FIRST

IGNORE ANYONE WHO DOESN'T WORSHIP YOU

ACCEPT LOVE ON YOUR OWN TERMS

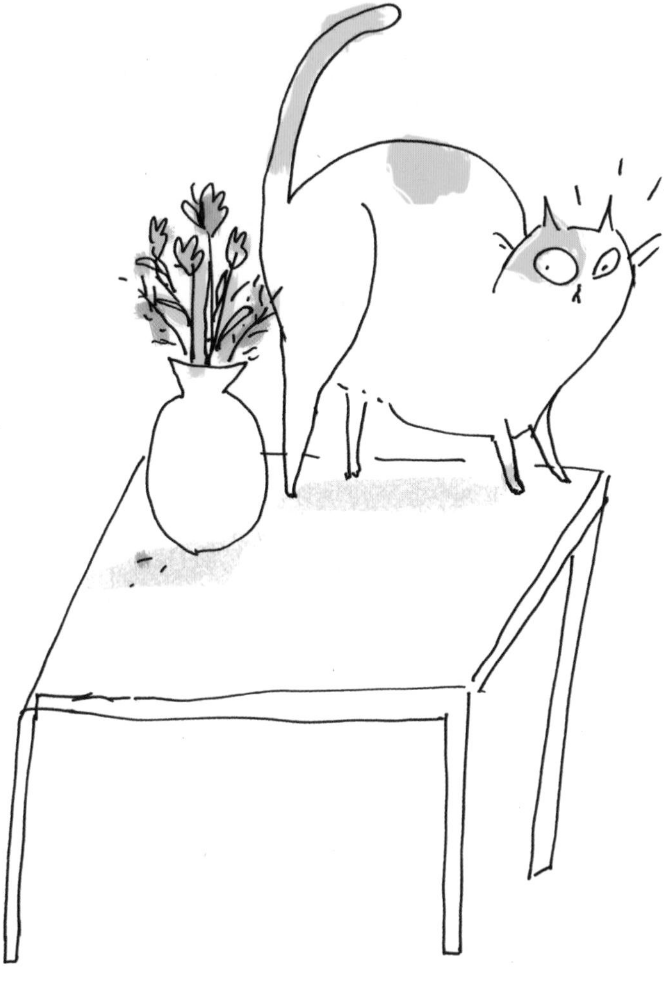

LOOK BEFORE YOU LEAP

DON'T BE AFRAID OF MICE

NEVER TRUST
A MAN WHO
DOESN'T
LIKE CATS

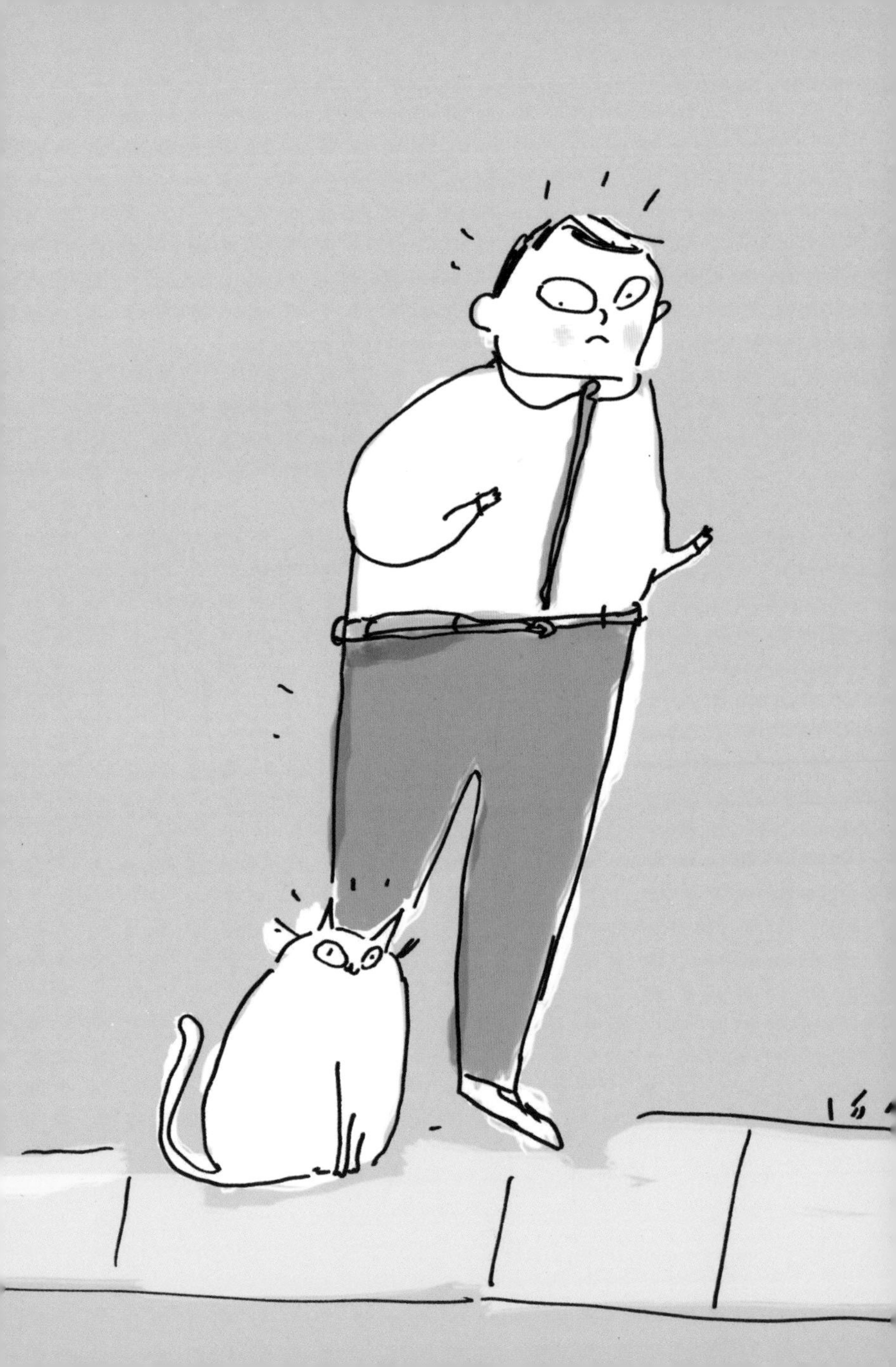

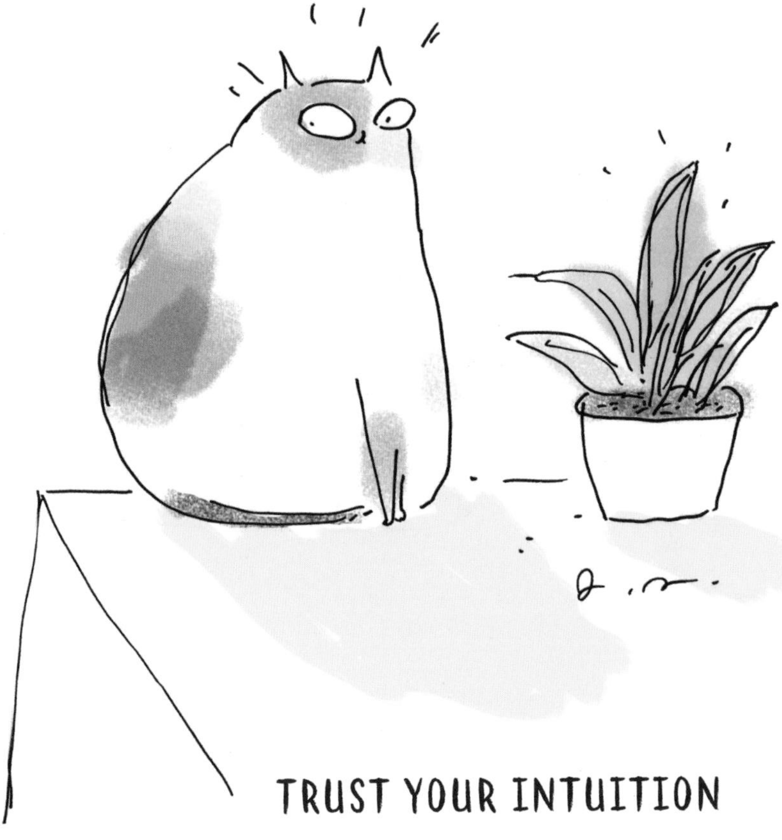

TRUST YOUR INTUITION

BE CURIOUS

BE YOURSELF

BE INDEPENDENT

BE ELUSIVE

TEST THE

BOUNDARIES

PRESERVE YOUR DIGNITY AT ALL TIMES

BE A GOOD LISTENER

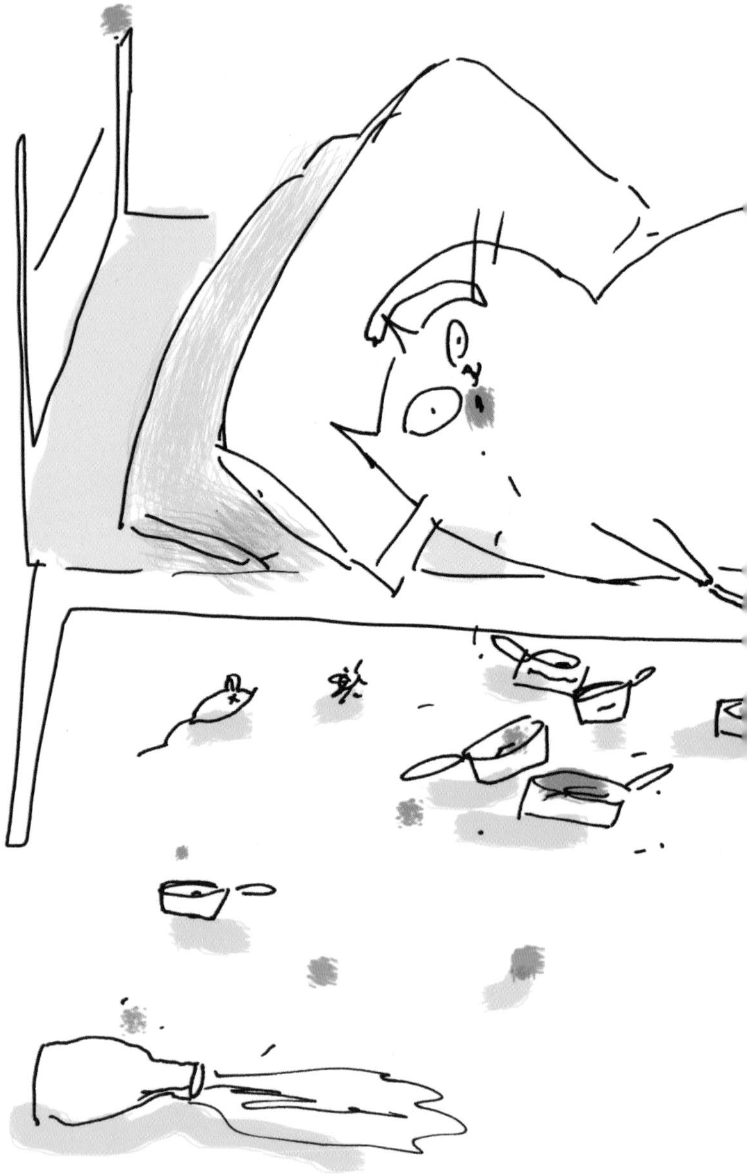

MAKE THE MOST OF YOUR NINE LIVES

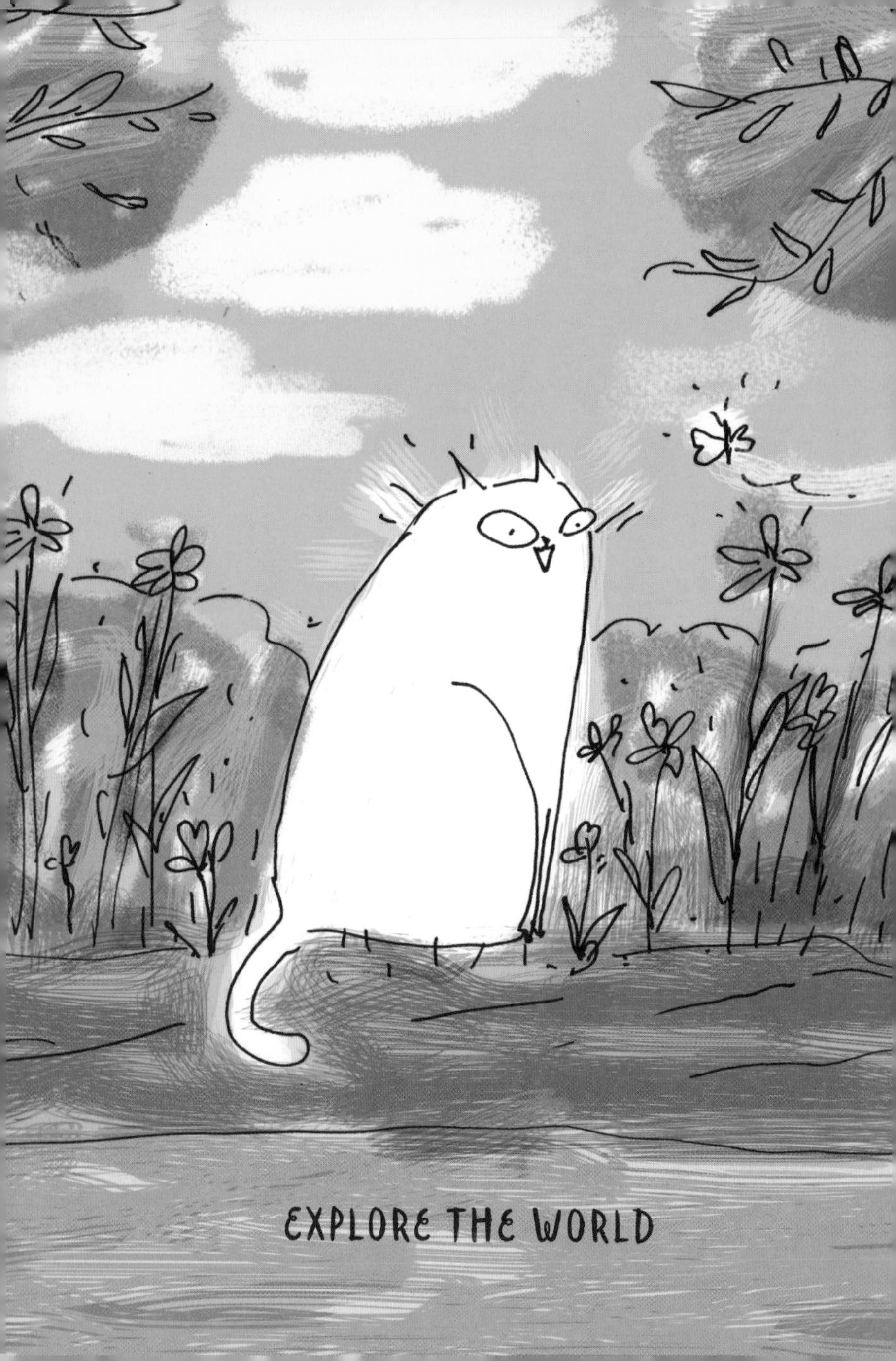
EXPLORE THE WORLD

YOU CAN NAP ANYWHERE

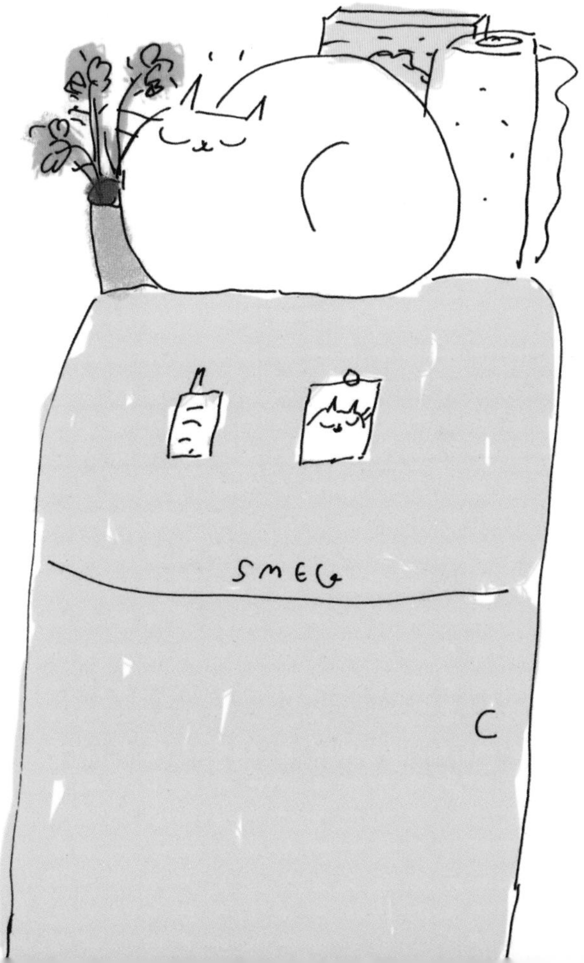
SMEG

LOOK AT THINGS FROM A
DIFFERENT PERSPECTIVE

DON'T WORRY WHAT
OTHERS THINK OF YOU

A HISS IS WORTH A
THOUSAND WORDS

BE EASILY ENTERTAINED

GET AWAY
WITH MURDER
BY LOOKING
CUTE

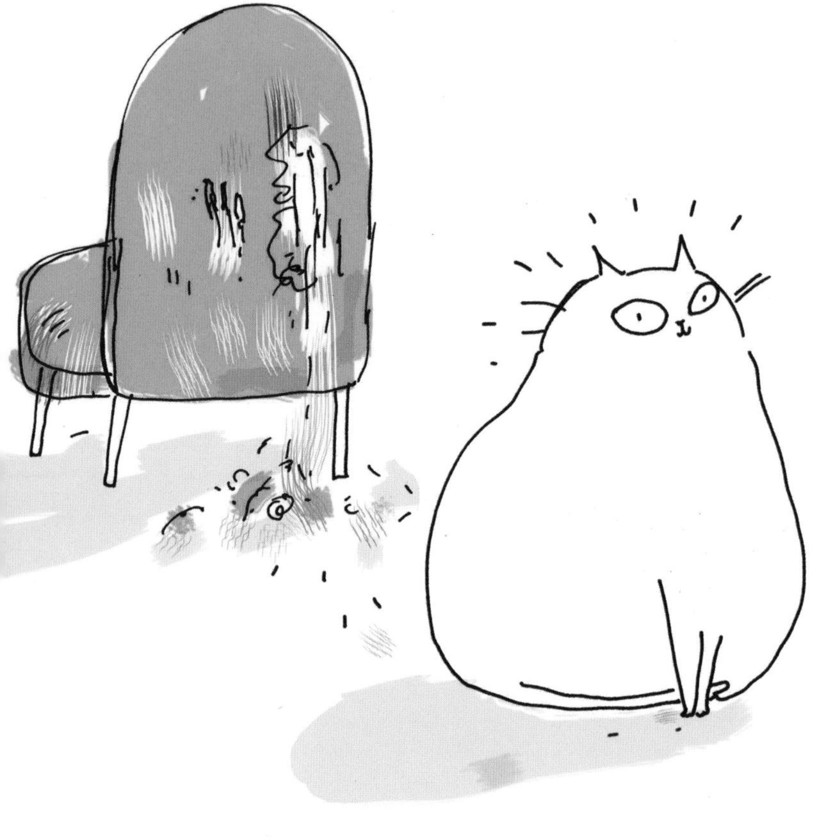

THE BEST SEAT IN THE HOUSE
IS THE ONE SOMEONE IS
ALREADY SITTING ON

THERE'S NOTHING BETTER
THAN A GOOD BOOK

LEARN TO MAKE YOURSELF AT-HOME WHEREVER YOU ARE

NEVER LOSE YOUR PLAYFULNESS

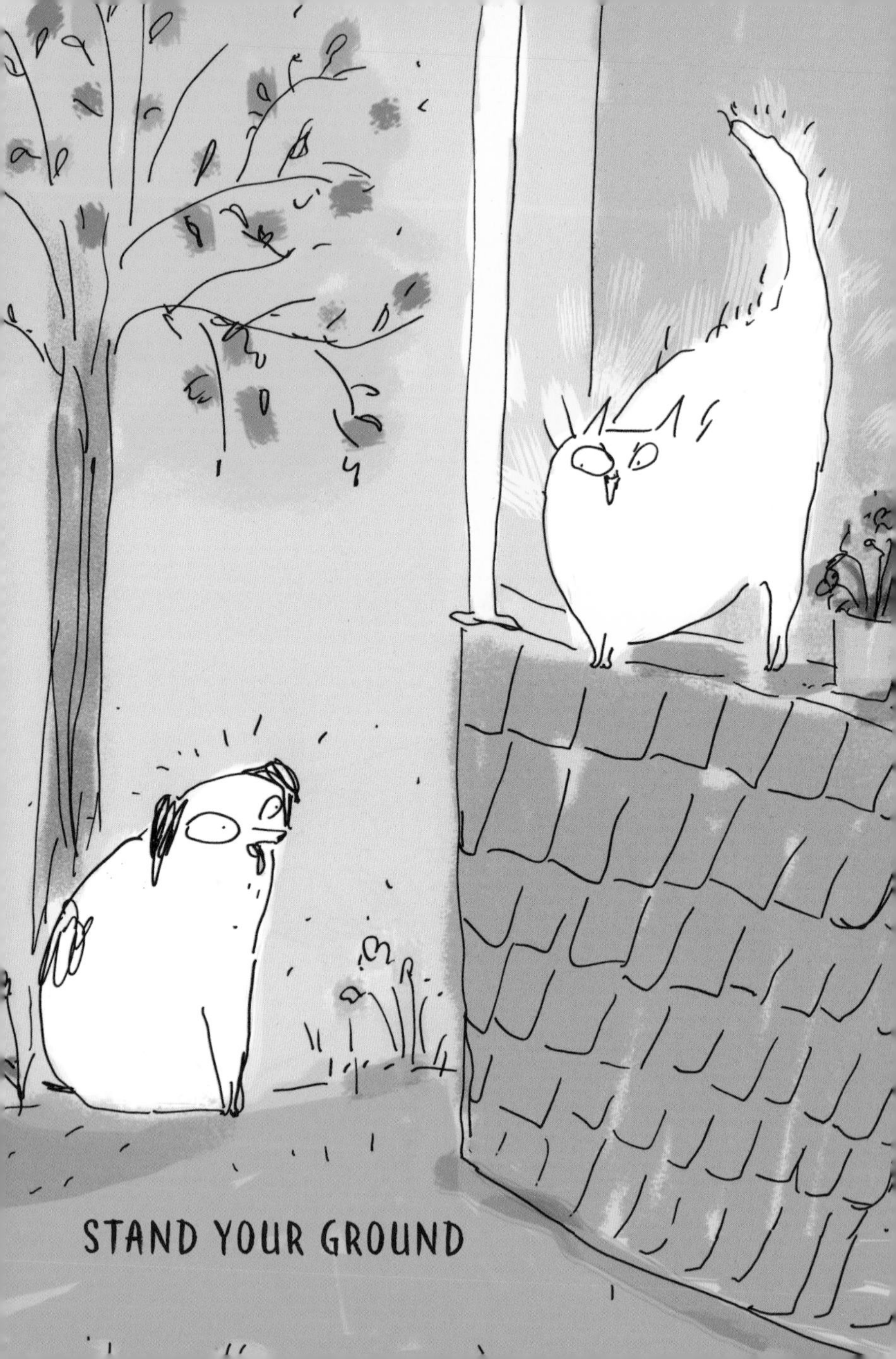
STAND YOUR GROUND

BE TAKEN
ON YOUR
OWN TERMS

ALWAYS GIVE GENEROUSLY

CHOOSE YOUR FRIENDS WISELY

BE SILLY . . . AND OFTEN

KEEP YOUR ENEMIES CLOSE

EMBRACE

YOUR

WEIRD

BE TOLERANT OF CHILDREN

CELEBRATE FAMILY MEALTIMES

IF YOU WANT SOMEONE'S ATTENTION,

SIT IN FRONT OF THE TV

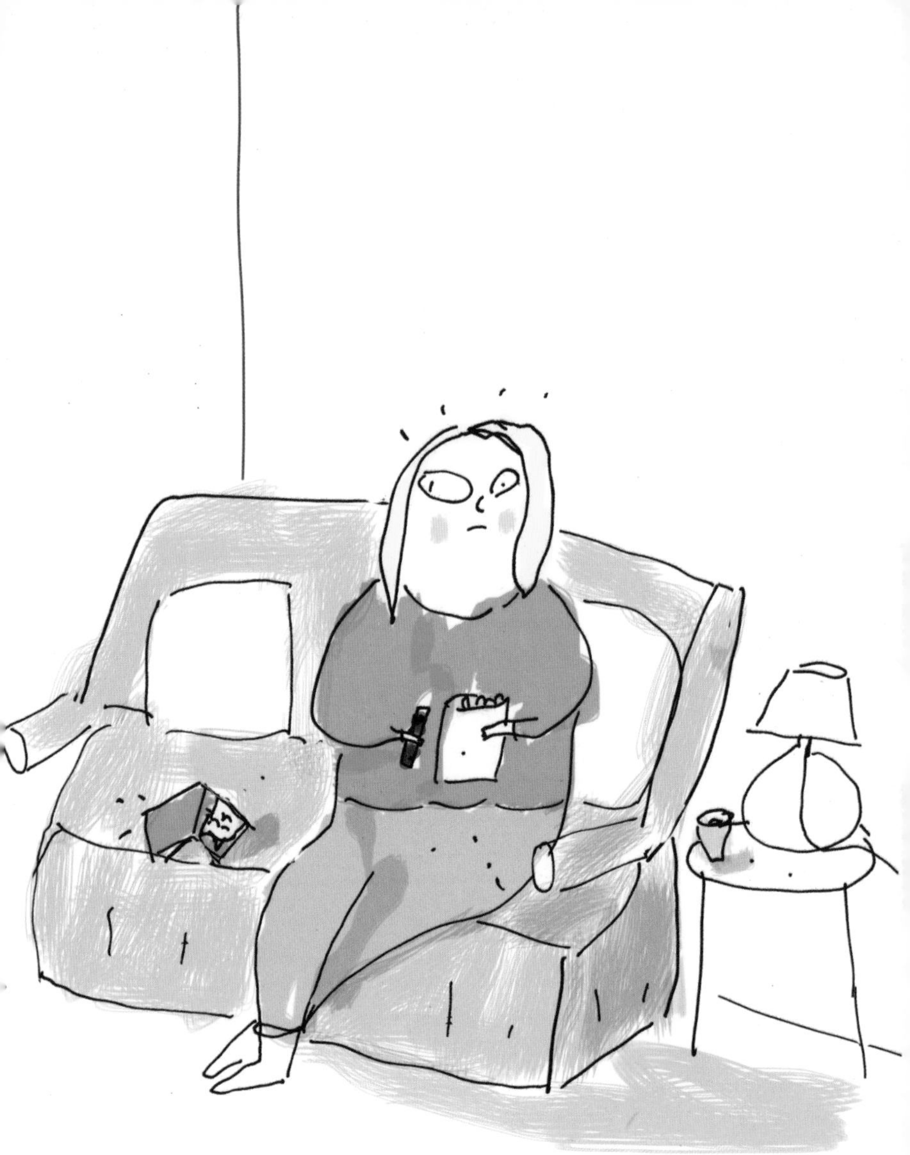

ALWAYS DEFEND YOUR HOME

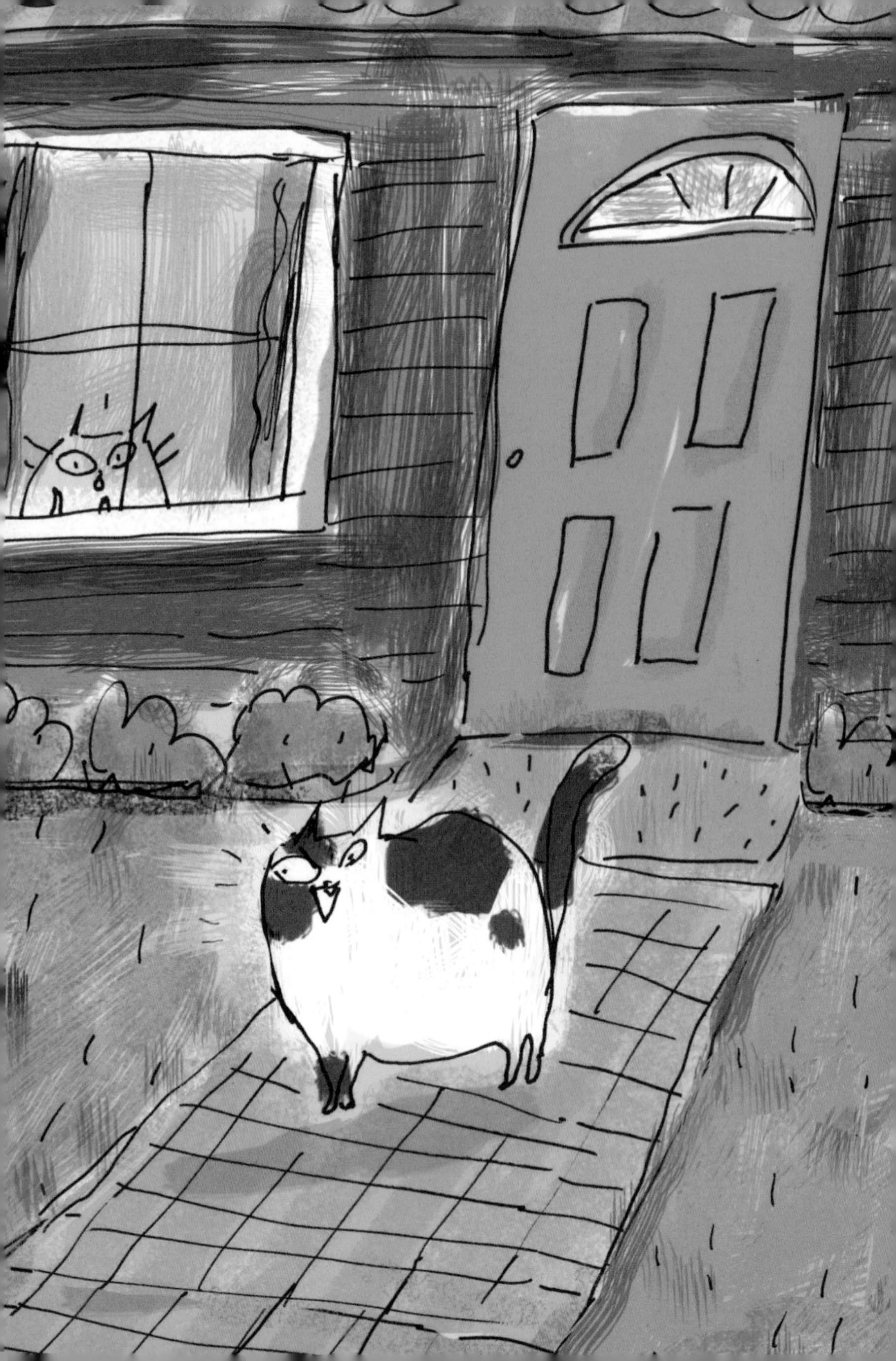

A CHAOTIC HOME IS A HAPPY HOME

BE THE CENTER OF
ATTENTION AT ANY COST

NEVER LET

ANYONE

DRESS YOU

SOMETIMES YOU WILL
LEAP AND FALL

... BUT YOU CAN STILL LAND ON YOUR FEET!

Artist and illustrator **Jamie Shelman** holds a degree in painting from the Rhode Island School of Design (RISD). She runs The Dancing Cat, an online stationery and print shop, and she is also a popular Etsy seller. Her muse (the neighbor's cat) waits at the window every morning to be let in, and then out, and then back in. She lives in Baltimore.

www.JamieShelman.com
@ thedancingcatart